COPING WITH THE AFTERMATH OF NATURAL DISASTERS

Lisa A. Crayton

Published in 2020 by The Rosen Publishing Group, Inc.
29 East 21st Street, New York, NY 10010

Copyright © 2020 by The Rosen Publishing Group, Inc.

First Edition

All rights reserved. No part of this book may be reproduced in any form without permission in writing from the publisher, except by a reviewer.

Library of Congress Cataloging-in-Publication Data

Names: Crayton, Lisa A., author.
Title: Coping with the aftermath of natural disasters / Lisa Crayton.
Description: New York : Rosen Publishing, 2020 | Series: Coping | Includes bibliographical references and index. | Audience: Grades 7-12.
Identifiers: LCCN 2019013683 | ISBN 9781725341326 (library binding) | ISBN 9781725341319 (paperback)
Subjects: LCSH: Disaster relief—Juvenile literature. | Disasters—Social aspects—Juvenile literature. | Community life—Juvenile literature.
Classification: LCC HV553 .C73 2019 | DDC 363.34/8—dc23
LC record available at https://lccn.loc.gov/2019013683

Manufactured in China

On the cover: Teens are important community members whose volunteer efforts, including cleanup, help communities effectively cope in the aftermath of natural disasters.

Some of the images in this book illustrate individuals who are models. The depictions do not imply actual situations or events.

CONTENTS

INTRODUCTION 4

CHAPTER ONE
Weather Watch 8

CHAPTER TWO
Disaster Relief 21

CHAPTER THREE
Water, Water Everywhere 35

CHAPTER FOUR
Snow Daze 46

CHAPTER FIVE
Shake, Rattle, Spin 57

CHAPTER SIX
Forest on Fire 70

CHAPTER SEVEN
Brighter Forecast 82

GLOSSARY 98

FOR MORE INFORMATION 100

FOR FURTHER READING 104

BIBLIOGRAPHY 105

INDEX 108

INTRODUCTION

Not more _____ ! Fill in the blank with a frequently occurring storm. Perhaps it's rain or snow. Or maybe it's a drought or heat wave. Depending on the time of year and an area's prevailing weather conditions, there are many different types of weather that become tiresome after happening over and over again. Such conditions cause school delays, traffic snafus, travel woes, and other everyday nuisances. Sometimes bothersome weather conditions morph into natural disasters.

A natural disaster is a devastating condition, often weather-related, that causes extensive damage to the environment and property. It also poses substantial risk of harm or death to people, pets, and wildlife. Tornadoes, floods, wildfires, hurricanes, and blizzards are familiar natural disasters that occur in many parts of the United States and Canada. Less familiar, but equally destructive, are volcano eruptions, tsunamis, and landslides.

Natural disasters are destructive. Much has been learned about them over the years, and technology has aided in the prediction and response time to some. Others do not conform

Concerned residents of Lagos, Nigeria, wade through high waters as they cope in the aftermath of devastating flooding from torrential rainfall.

to predictions. They may last longer, cause more damage, or harm more lives than expected. Still others strike with little or no warning. That surprise factor increases the chance for greater devastation and harm.

Facing the challenges of a natural disaster begins with information and preparation. During a natural disaster, the most important factor is survival. Minimizing property and environmental damage is a close second goal. The next phase is coping with its aftermath. The aftermath reveals how bad the situation is. It is difficult to imagine how quickly things change so dramatically. The extent of damage and harm varies depending on the type of natural disaster. Flattened homes, uprooted trees, crushed vehicles, and downed power lines, for example, are common after a hurricane or tornado.

In the aftermath, people want to get their lives back on track. But how long it will take for a community to get back to normal operations varies with each natural disaster. A lot depends on the extent of damage and whether roads are clear for emergency workers to do their jobs. For example, if electrical equipment such as a power grid is damaged, it can take weeks for an area to get its electricity restored.

Overall, life is different after a natural disaster. A community will not operate or exist in the way it did prior to a natural disaster. Residents will need time to mourn the loss of loved ones. Neighbors who are injured may need continued medical care. Meanwhile, lots of ongoing activity will be required to get homes, schools, roads, and other affected structures in tip-top shape.

Tough decisions have to be made. Residents may be displaced for weeks or months. Business owners may be unable to open their establishments for a while. Those unable to rebuild a home or business may struggle with whether to permanently relocate. The decisions may not be easy, but they have to be made. Why? Because natural disasters pose a challenge to the entire world. They come in different forms and happen throughout the year. Some are preventable. Others can't be avoided. For these reasons, it is important to know how to cope in the aftermath of a natural disaster.

CHAPTER ONE

Weather Watch

Facing natural disasters is a scary prospect. Yet, there is no avoiding them. Disasters can happen anywhere, at any time of day or night. The time frame—or window—to respond depends on how much advance notice people are given. Sometimes it's unbelievably short. Five minutes. That's all some Alabama residents had before tornadoes swept through Lee County, Alabama, in March 2019, according to a CNN .com article by Susannah Cullinane and Joe Sterling. Sadly, twenty-three people died. The authors noted that the reported deaths "marked the deadliest day of tornadoes in Alabama since [a] tornado that killed more than 200 people in 2011." The risk to people's lives is what makes a natural disaster so traumatic. Added to that risk is the structural and financial impact to communities.

When a tornado rips through a community, it poses a tremendous risk of structural damage to homes, schools, businesses, and other property.

Up Close

A natural disaster is a large-scale event that poses a significant risk to people, property, and the environment. Hurricanes and tornadoes demolish homes, uproot trees, crush vehicles, and down power lines. Floods drop massive amounts of water into areas, submerging streets, roads, homes, and more. Avalanches dump excessive amounts of snow, blanketing resort areas, towns, and other affected areas. Meanwhile, wildfires strip forests and towns, creating hazardous heat and smoke conditions.

Varying Causes

Extreme weather and people cause natural disasters. Common types of extreme weather include those mentioned here—floods, hurricanes, tornadoes, and blizzards. These batter cities, states, and nations. Usually students are most familiar with those in their area, those where relatives and friends live, or those in places they've visited.

Weather-related disasters can't be prevented—or avoided. For example, no one can put a cap on a volcano and stop it from blowing! Similarly, a drought can't be stopped. If there is no rain for a prolonged time, a drought will occur. These natural disasters are particularly troublesome.

People also cause disasters. They may accidentally forget to do something, or they may not complete a task. For example, discarded cigarettes and fireworks can spark a small fire that expands into a massive fire event. So can a campfire that a person forgets to fully extinguish before leaving an area. Such wildfires should never happen—but they do. Frequently.

When people commit certain crimes, they also cause natural disasters. For example, they may deliberately ignore a burn ban and start a fire. Or they may deliberately commit arson by setting fire to something. If such fires spread, particularly in wildlands, they result in devastating natural disasters.

Who's Affected?

Natural disasters are traumatic events. Occurring throughout the world every year, they turn a normal day into a trouble-filled week, month, or year. They affect people of all races, ages, and economic backgrounds. Residents in affected areas are impacted by natural disasters. They also impact tourists visiting an affected area for holidays or other special occasions. Natural disasters hinder travel. Visitors already at their destination may not be able to return home for days, or longer. Others may be stranded temporarily at airports because of grounded flights caused by inclement weather.

The Price Tag

Natural disasters are costly! It is expensive to clean up and repair communities and infrastructures after an event. From 1980 to 2018, the total costs related to weather and climate disasters equaled more than $1.6 trillion, according to an article on the National Centers for Environmental Information (NCEI) website, ncdc.noaa.gov. The agency is part of the National Oceanic and Atmospheric Administration

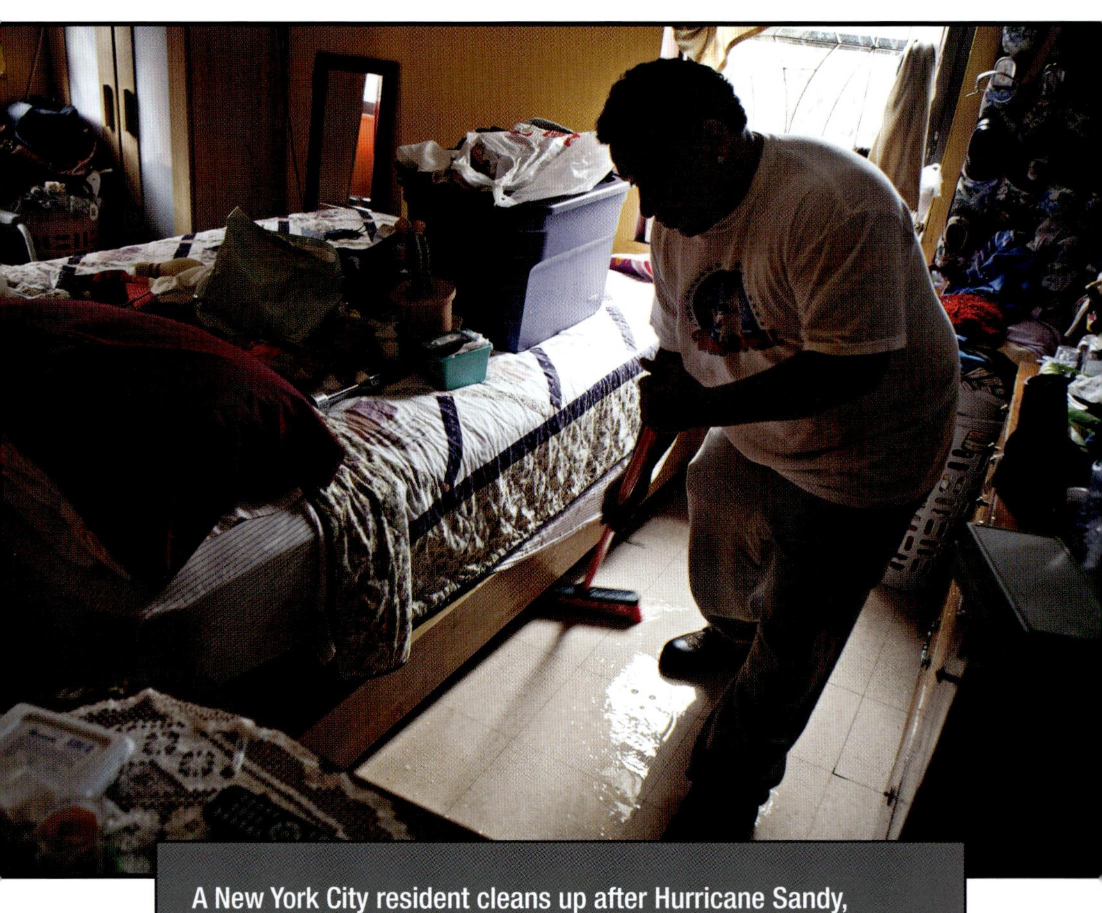

A New York City resident cleans up after Hurricane Sandy, which slammed the East Coast in 2012 and killed more than thirty people.

(NOAA). According to its website, the NCEI "tracks and evaluates climate events in the U.S. and globally that have great economic and societal impacts." In 2018, according to NCEI, 247 people died from events that cost more than $1 billion each.

Compassionate Financial Help

Natural disasters adversely affect low-income people because they may live in communities that are not in the best shape. Buildings and roads, for example, may not be in prime condition to withstand the onslaught of a hurricane, tornado, or other natural disaster. In addition, low-income residents may not be able to afford much-needed supplies, medication, or money for rebuilding.

Government agencies, relief groups, faith-based organizations, and other concerned entities try to make it financially easier for low-income residents. They want people to know that compassionate help is available. Using these community resources can help families better cope in the aftermath of a natural disaster.

A Quick Glance

According to the NCEI, the fourteen events in 2018 that cost more than $1 billion each were split as follows: one drought, eight severe storms, two tropical cyclones, one wildfire, and two winter storms. The 2018 events reveal the varying nature of disasters. Many more occurred that caused millions of dollars in damage.

Some of the more familiar natural disasters are discussed in detail in other chapters. There is, perhaps, a greater chance for students to experience those while at home or while visiting loved ones. There is, perhaps, a less likely chance they will experience others, such as landslides and volcanic eruptions. Here's a brief look at those two types of natural disasters.

Mud Mess

Heavy rains can cause the soil to slip, creating a landslide. A common type of landslide is a mudslide, also called a debris flow. Generally, a landslide is a mix of wet dirt, rocks, soil, and other things that tumble down slopes, hillsides, mountains, and other steep land. In addition to rain, fire can cause a landslide. Because of the changed conditions of the environment after a wildfire, uprooted plants and trees no longer anchor soil. Landslides are possible in those cases.

Regardless of its origin, a landslide can start slowly or quickly. When it's fast, massive amounts of mudslide can pick up and/or mix with any debris in its path. Landslides are powerful forces. Nothing is safe in their path! They can carry away buildings, trees, people, and animals. Large boulders can also be swept up and carried along. A landslide or mudslide can be deadly. According to an article on WeatherWizKids .com, an average of twenty-five to fifty people die from mudslides every year.

When people live or visit a landslide-prone area, it's important for them to be aware of what's happening with the land during wet weather. As with other natural disasters, pay attention to and follow any weather warnings or evacuation orders. In the aftermath of a landslide, call for help if people are trapped. Trying to help rescue them is not wise as it could put you in danger. If it has happened elsewhere in the community, stay clear from all affected areas, as it is possible to get hurt or trapped in the aftermath of a landslide.

Hot Stuff

Natural Resources Canada provides an easy-to-understand definition of a volcano on its website, chis .nrcan.gc.ca: "an opening in the earth's crust through which lava, volcanic ash, and gases escape." On Earth, volcanoes exist around the world. According to a US Geological Survey (USGS) website article on active volcanoes, "There are 169 potentially active volcanoes in the United States" and "1500 worldwide."

In the United States, most people only associate Hawaii with volcanoes. Among its many volcanoes

Erupting volcanoes spew dangerous gases and other materials that are harmful to people, animals, and the environment. Because of that, it is essential to follow any evacuation orders.

is Mauna Loa. According to the USGS, Mauna Loa rises more than 13,100 feet (4 kilometers) above sea level and is the most active volcano on Earth. The USGS also explains that Mauna Loa "covers half of the Island of Hawai'i and by itself amounts to about 85 percent of the area of all the other Hawaiian Islands combined."

Volcanoes can be very dangerous because when they erupt, they spew gases, hot ash, and rocks. Those move very rapidly, causing damage on contact. They also affect air quality, which can make it dangerous for people to breathe. Volcanoes can spark other natural disasters, including earthquakes and tsunamis. They

Fun with Science

Every year, students in different grades must complete a science project. Doing so can be a fun way to experience science close up. Projects featuring natural disasters or other weather-related topics can be impressive. Select a topic and develop it into a project that informs—and possibly entertains. Volcano-related projects usually do both. People are drawn to its bubbles, as they mimic a real eruption. As always when working with science projects: remember, safety first. Use caution when building and displaying any project, especially when getting help from classmates, teachers, or a parent or guardian.

In some school districts, science projects are big deals. Students compete for awards at their school. Then they compete in science fairs against other students in their district or state. In some cases, students who do not have to do a project for classwork can still enter a competition and represent their school.

are not all bad. The ash, for example, is beneficial for soil.

Scientists study volcanoes but can't always predict when one will erupt. They were able to successfully predict the 1980 eruption of Mount St. Helens in Washington, which helped saved lives. Nonetheless, more than fifty people died from the natural disaster. Getting and staying away from an erupting volcano is vital for safety. In the aftermath, it's important to steer clear of the area until it has been deemed safe to visit.

Volcanoes are not unique to Earth. According to the National Aeronautics and Space Administration (NASA), volcanoes exist on other planets! Extinct volcanoes exist on Venus and Mars, and active volcanoes exist "on some of the moons of Jupiter, Saturn, and Neptune."

Impact on Animals

Like people, animals are affected by natural disasters. Wildlife, cattle, and farm animals can die or be hurt. In addition, cats, dogs, and other pets can:

- Get hurt or killed while outside during a disaster
- Get hurt or killed in damaged property
- Get lost or go missing in the aftermath of a natural disaster

When a natural disaster strikes, people are forced to rapidly leave areas. Sometimes, their pets must be put in animal shelters until a storm ends.

- Need rescuing when a dwelling is damaged
- Suffer storm-related stress symptoms and require medical care

Getting animals the help they need in the aftermath of a natural disaster is essential. Also, pets may need care or housing. Often, many lost pets are housed temporarily in shelters until their owners are located. Fostering or adopting an animal is a way to help.

Fostering an animal provides needed shelter and care until it is reunited with its owners. Some owners, however, have to make the difficult decision not to retrieve animals when they no longer have permanent space for them. Pet adoptions are a great way to help those animals find new, loving homes in the aftermath of a natural disaster.

Clearly, a natural disaster can dramatically change the way individuals, families, and communities operate. Learning more about these situations prepares the way for survival, and knowing how to cope in the aftermath helps people and communities bounce back from adversity.

Disaster Relief

CHAPTER TWO

A natural disaster triggers an emergency for everyone and everything in its path. Disaster relief begins immediately in the aftermath. It is a race against time to save lives, property, and the environment. Teamwork is essential. As the familiar adage notes, "teamwork makes the dream work." It comes into play as people work together to help.

Those skilled in disaster relief train throughout the year for such emergencies. Service providers, meanwhile, focus on providing assistance throughout the year, making it easy for them to act. All told, it is a coordinated effort. Lots of activity focuses on making thing better—quickly. The overall goal is to save, protect, and restore. Short- and long-term services assist those impacted. Here's how it works.

Natural disasters strike quickly. When they are over, the extent of the devastation is clear. Help

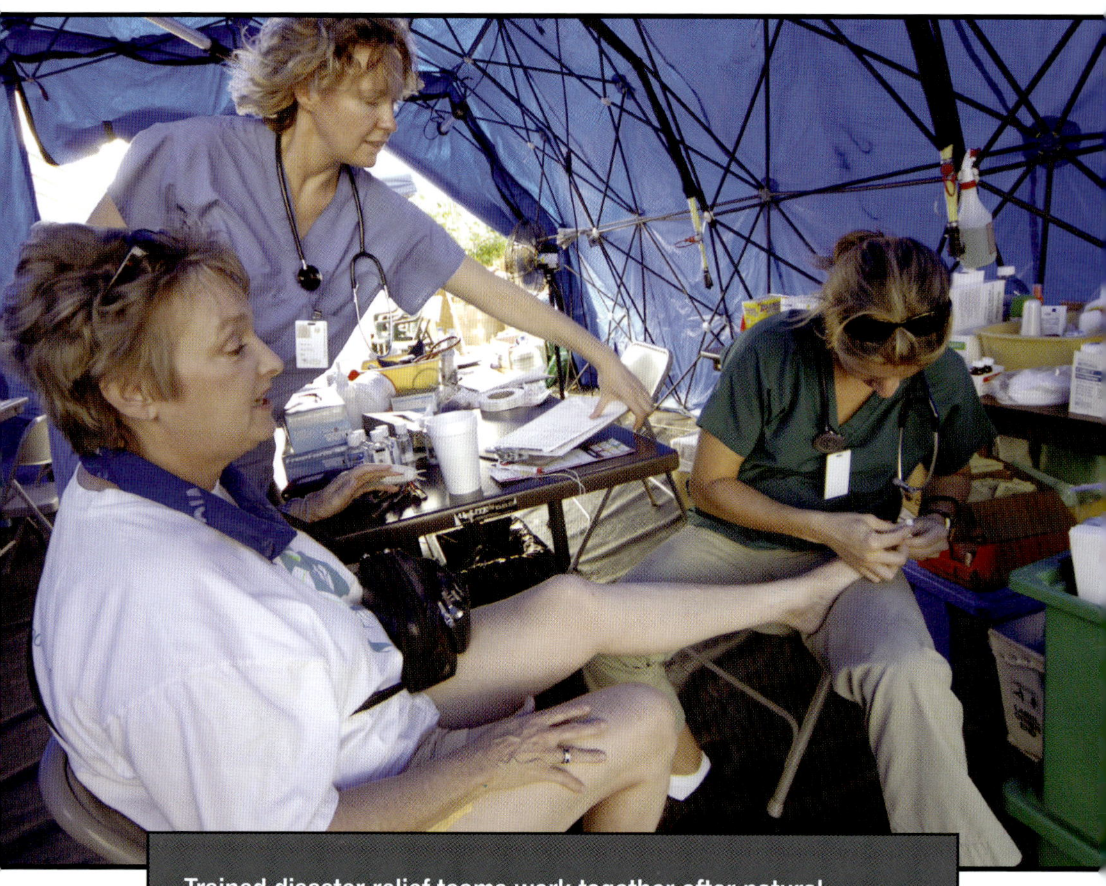

Trained disaster relief teams work together after natural disasters to provide routine and emergency medical services to injured residents.

comes in from various sources. Providing medical care to injured people tops the lists. Others help with the rescue and recovery effort for people trapped or killed. Others work on utilities, such as restoring electricity or cutting off gas to homes and businesses to prevent natural gas explosions.

Meeting basic needs is a priority. Items such as clothing and food are urgently needed, so workers assure these items are on hand. Some helpers concentrate on finding temporary, safe, comfortable places to live for those affected. Animals are not overlooked. Pets and other animals may need medical care, shelter, or just a kind human touch. Relief workers make sure animals are taken care of with basic needs and loving attention.

All Hands on Deck

Disaster relief is an enormous task! In truth, a lot of little things are needed to meet big needs. No one person or organization can provide it all. That's where teamwork comes in. The response to a natural disaster requires lots of hands on deck and lots of money and resources.

Some helpers are victims. They include neighbors on the scene who call for help, encourage injured friends, or lend a hand to remove debris. Others are first responders. Those workers include law enforcement, fire personnel, and medical crews who provide specific help based on their job specialty. Still others are employees and volunteers with disaster relief companies and organizations.

Local, state, and federal government can play key roles in meeting residents' needs. They assess and address damage resulting from a natural disaster. Each has an allotted budget for routine and emergency services. When a local government can't handle the cost of responding to an emergency or needs extra helpers, it seeks help from its state. When a state can't help, it appeals to the federal government for assistance.

Local Assistance

The goal is to share responsibility and costs associated with natural disasters. Local government will step in first because its role is to help people in its area. A city or county may provide emergency shelter, food, or other essential items. It will offer information and resources, like how to get emergency financial help, and oversee the removal of trees and debris. It also makes sure bridges and roads are repaired. If needed, it steps in to ensure utility companies and other providers restore services to residents as swiftly as possible. There are many other things a local government does after a disaster.

Locally, school districts pitch in. School employees, such as educators and administrators, and students are affected by natural disasters. Schools also may be damaged or destroyed. Thus, school systems offer useful information and resources. They let people know about changes in school scheduling. They also tell others about temporary relocation of classes when schools can't be used because of damage, flooding, or other problems. Some school systems agree to use select schools as temporary shelters. People can go there and safely wait out a storm or sleep there overnight if needed.

Fighting wildfires is a team effort, often requiring local, state, and national departments to work together against quick winds and destructive flames.

State Aid

State agencies help the entire state. In many cases, they partner with local government officials to do so. At other times, affected states will receive help from other states. Many states have trained disaster workers who can quickly organize and travel to affected areas. These courageous teams rush in to help, often arriving within hours or days of a natural disaster. For example, Virginia may send its specially trained firefighters to help fight wildfires in California.

States also seek federal aid when needed. Governors have the power to declare a state of emergency, which is a disaster-related status that indicates the amount of damage or loss of life is expected to be substantial. It paves the way for the state to step in and provide needed financial or other assistance to affected areas—or to request federal assistance to do so. A state of emergency makes it easier to force residents to stay indoors and/or off roads. People do not like curfews, but staying indoors increases safety and helps workers do their jobs. It also reduces the number of potential crimes.

National Help

The federal government has an agency dedicated to disaster relief. It is the Federal Emergency

Management Agency (FEMA), and it was established on April 1, 1979. Helping people before, during, and after disasters is its mission, according to FEMA.gov. FEMA has regional offices throughout the nation and makes it easier for US citizens to get the help and resources they need. For example, it provides financial grants to help homeowners rebuild or secure affordable

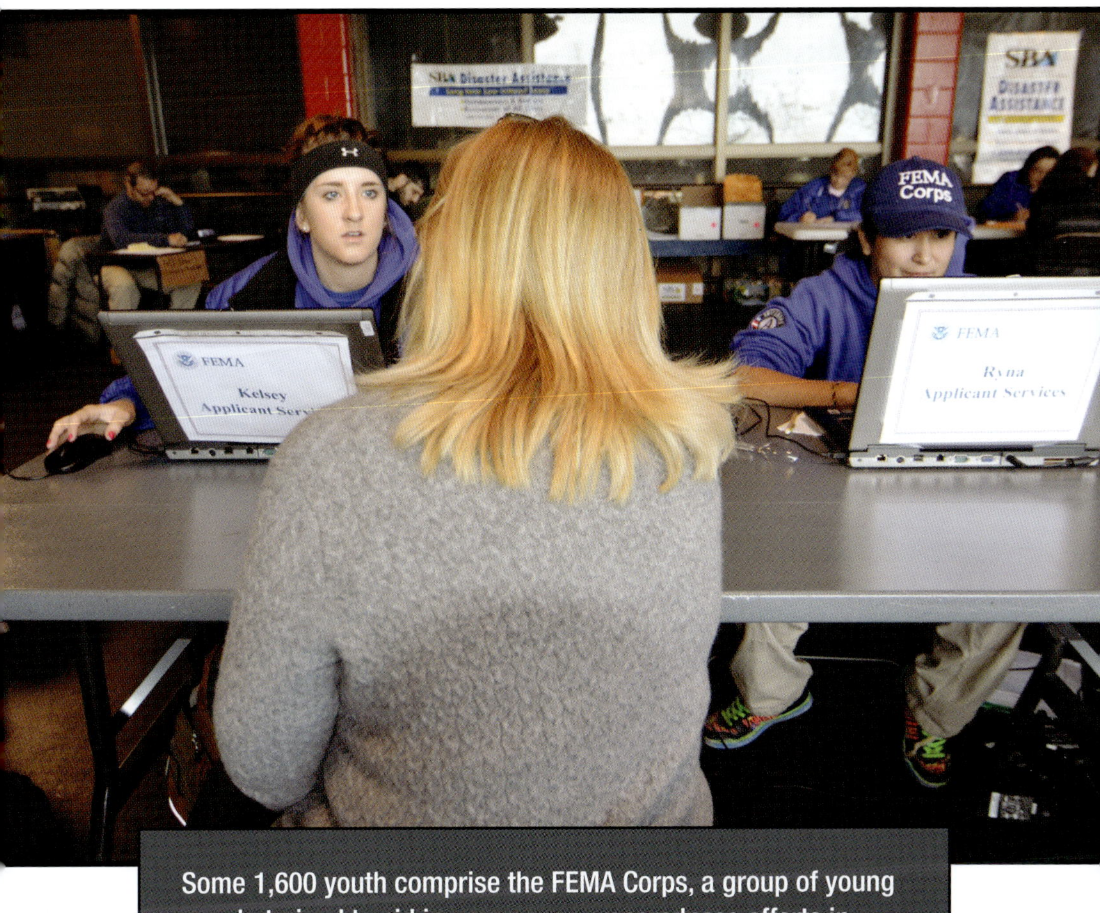

Some 1,600 youth comprise the FEMA Corps, a group of young people trained to aid in emergency preparedness efforts in their communities.

loans to help pay for fixing or rebuilding damaged property. FEMA is also the agency that coordinates federal government involvement during a national emergency. The president of the United States declares a national emergency in extreme circumstances, such as after the September 11, 2001, terrorist attack.

FEMA's READY.gov website has lots of educational material about natural disasters. Site visitors can learn about the various types of disasters, why they happen, how to respond in the aftermath, and how to prepare financially. It also includes information on how students in grades eight through twelve can join its Youth Preparedness Council. The council is for youth leaders who are committed to community service or who want to help with emergency preparedness efforts locally and nationally. Check READY.gov for application information and deadlines.

Other Helpers

Disaster relief is also provided by coordinated response teams from nonprofit organizations, such as the American Red Cross and the United Way. Like governmental agencies, these provide information or resources that help people obtain:

Blood Donations Save Lives

Injuries from natural disasters vary. As the number of injured people rises, so does the need and demand for blood. In some cases, the levels in an area may dip so low that an urgent call goes out for donors as blood donations save lives!

Only healthy teens and adults can donate blood. In most cases, students over seventeen years old can do so without parental consent; sixteen-year-old students can do so with consent. Restrictions apply concerning the frequency of donations. Weight and height restrictions also apply to potential student donors.

- Clothing
- Food
- Temporary shelter
- Financial help
- Other assistance

The Red Cross also helps to alert residents about urgent needs for blood donations.

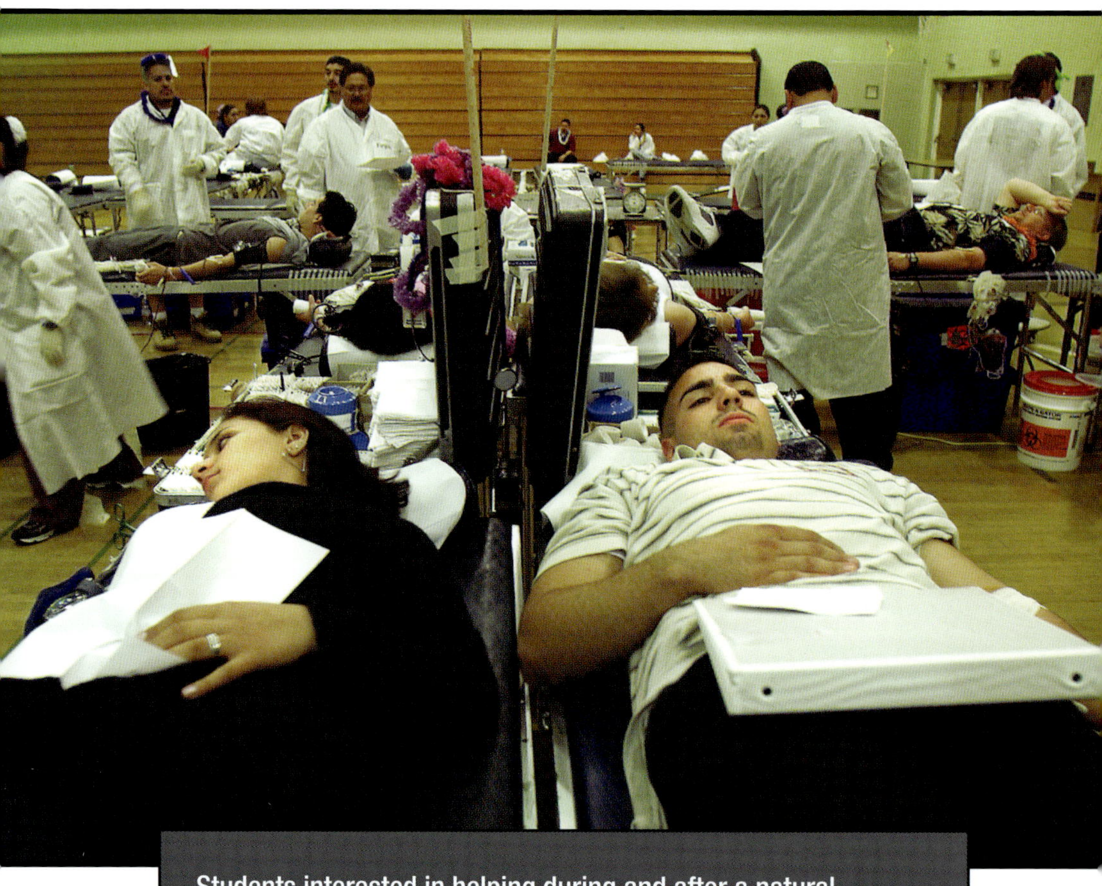

Students interested in helping during and after a natural disaster can donate blood to keep the community's blood supply at an adequate level for injured residents.

Role of the Media

The media is an important part of society. Its news coverage about incidents keeps people informed. Before a natural disaster, the media shares the impending event, its track, and expected impact. Then, as a disaster unfolds, the media offers critical updates and news about evacuation orders. To stay safe and informed, tune in to news stories on social media, the radio, or the television. Don't rely solely on TV, computers, or cell phones, though, as these items can lose power. Always keep a battery-operated radio or TV ready for use in case of an emergency.

In the aftermath of a disaster, the media serves the community by providing important information about disaster relief, including cleanup efforts, where to find shelter or financial assistance, and whether schools and businesses are open, closed, or operating on a delayed status. Media outlets will also share information about residents who died, heroic efforts during a disaster, and other information of particular interest to readers and viewers.

Local media usually first reports about an incident. However, the news quickly spreads to wider areas. State, national, and international media covers disasters outside their areas because such events are of widespread interest. Also, the way a disaster occurs, its impact, and related costs can provide crucial information for other states' or countries' future responses to natural disasters.

Lasting Relief

Coping in the aftermath means receiving—or giving—assistance. Without disaster relief, people

Communities set up short-term shelters in weather-resistant buildings, such as convention centers, to provide housing in the aftermath of natural disasters.

and communities would suffer without any hope of recovering. Thus, disaster relief serves as an important tool for coping in the aftermath of a natural disaster.

Short-term, immediate relief is needed, but long-term relief is also important. A temporary shelter such as a school gymnasium obviously is not meant to shelter people long-term. Rather, people will eventually need more permanent housing. Other needs throughout the affected area must also be addressed. When people team up to provide food, shelter, clothing, blood, and transportation, they help their neighbors overcome the affect of natural disasters. When local, state, and federal agencies provide other resources, including financial assistance, lasting relief becomes a living reality and aids in the coping process.

Myths & FACTS

Myth: Taping windows is an effective way to prepare for a hurricane.

Fact: Taping does not prevent windows from breaking during a hurricane.

Myth: Standing water from a natural disaster is safe to wade in or drive through.

Fact: Never walk or drive through standing water, as its depth can't be fully known. Instead, "turn around, don't drown."

Myth: Coping with the aftermath of a natural disaster is a quick and easy process.

Fact: Since every natural disaster is different, it is impossible to predict how long it will take for a person, family, or community to cope.

CHAPTER THREE

Water, Water Everywhere

Hurricane Maria barreled toward Puerto Rico in September 2017. It boasted sustained winds of 155 mph (249 kmh) and was expected to cause catastrophic damage. It slammed into the island on September 20, quickly living up to predictions. Hurricane Maria demolished businesses, homes, and other structures, bringing extensive flooding to the entire island. Trees toppled everywhere, as the oversaturated ground could not hold the trees in place.

Making matters worse, the hurricane knocked out the island's entire electrical grid and thrust residents into darkness. Residents, schools, places of worship, and businesses were without power for weeks. Even the street lights were out!

Simple tasks, such as cooking, bathing, shopping, and sleeping comfortably at home, became difficult. Telephone service was also impacted, and

The NASA Earth Observatory captured Hurricane Maria's strength and intensity; the natural disaster caused significant damage to Puerto Rico and other areas.

relief efforts were hampered by the conditions on the island. Bringing food and supplies was not an easy task.

In its report about the natural disaster, CNN .com quoted a spokesperson for the governor of Puerto Rico named Mr. Carlos Mercader. "This is total devastation," he said, adding, "This is something of historic proportions." All told, more than three thousand people died as a result of Hurricane Maria, which will long be remembered for its devastation. It was the worst storm on the island since 1933 and, even years after the horrific natural disaster, Puerto Rico still has not fully recovered.

Understanding Weather

Natural disasters like Hurricane Maria thrust weather into the news. All over the world, people pay attention to what is happening, watching the fierce impact it can make. But it can also be an icebreaker topic for a conversation. Talking about the weather helps people get over awkward moments, such as riding in elevators or attending a party with strangers. It is also discussed while people shop and run errands throughout the day. Weather is on most people's minds because it affects daily clothing choices, activities, transportation, and more.

Weather basically refers to the air. Temperature, on the other hand, refers to how cold or hot the air is. Temperature varies based on different factors, including the time of year and location where a person is on a given day. The temperature fluctuates throughout the day. Weather also can vary throughout a day or from day today. Seasonal changes occur because of how Earth is positioned compared to the sun.

At its best, weather is beneficial for people, vegetation, trees, and animals. It provides needed sunlight and water to help living things thrive. At its worst, weather is destructive, causing harm to people, animals, and the environment. Natural disasters are the most extreme weather conditions experienced around the world. Because they can't be avoided, it's important to learn more about them and how to cope in the aftermath of different types of natural disasters.

Stormy Weather

Tropical storms take different forms. They include hurricanes, cyclones, and tsunamis. They commonly are stormy weather conditions accompanied by destructive rain and winds. They often cause major flooding in affected areas. Such storms are extreme weather conditions. Residents are alerted to approaching tropical storms through news outlets, emergency alerts sent to mobile devices, and alerts on NOAA Weather Radio All Hazards (NWR). NWR gets weather-related information from the National Weather Service and then broadcasts it on a 24/7 basis. The NOAA issues watches, warnings, and local updates. A watch alerts residents of a storm threat or chance occurrence. If the storm comes, it will happen within a forty-eight-hour time frame. A

Status Update: Safe!

During natural disasters, social media users stay glued to their favorite platforms, hoping to read posts or see pictures of friends, relatives, neighbors, and coworkers. Affected local residents often provide detailed, first-hand information about what is happening on the ground in real time.

(continued on the next page)

Stay in the know by signing up for text messages for current weather conditions, emergency services, and other reliable information needed when disaster strikes.

(continued from the previous page)

Social media networks have attempted to make such information easier to share. For example, Facebook encourages use of its "Marked Safe" option during a crisis. Users click a link that designates them safe during a specific disaster. It's a quick and easy way to notify others and alleviate concerns.

watch notifies residents of a nearby tropical storm. As the storm approaches, the NOAA will issue local updates to help residents be prepared and informed.

Understanding Hurricanes

As a tropical storm, a hurricane is known for strong winds clocking 74 mph (119 kmh) or higher, soaking rains, and enormous waves. They are also common in certain bodies of water, particularly the North Atlantic Ocean and the eastern Pacific Ocean. Others begin in the Gulf of Mexico or the Caribbean Sea. Hurricanes swirl rapidly while traveling in a counter-clockwise pattern around its center—its "eye." In photographs, the center looks somewhat like a human eye and is a fearsome sight. According to the "Frequently Asked Questions" section of the

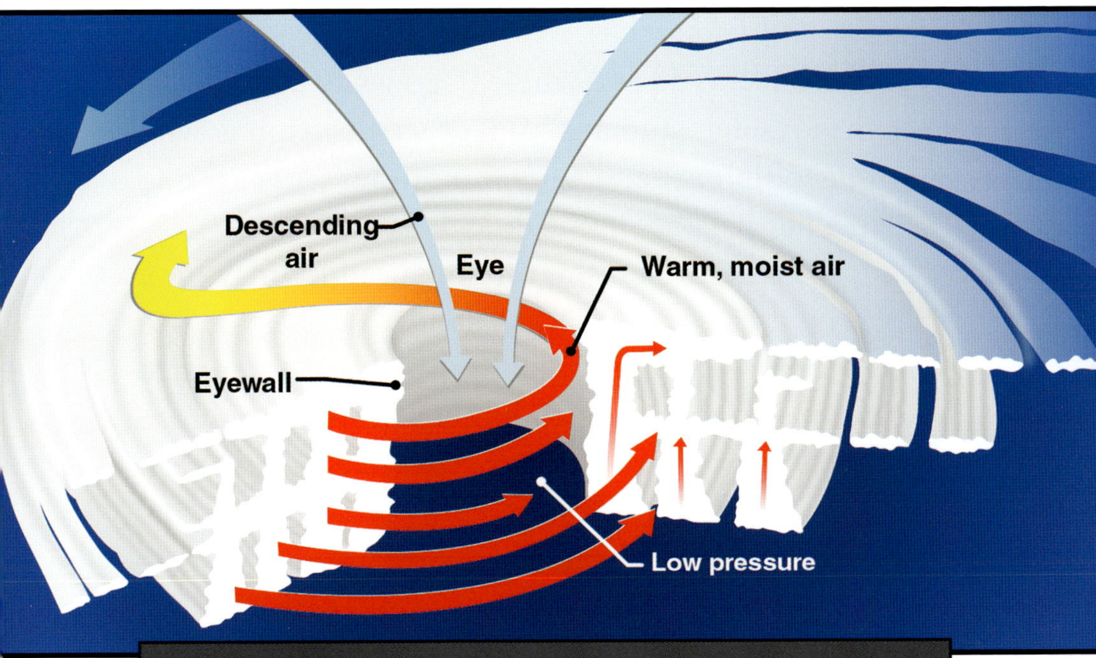

Using reputable online sources, such as NASA's website (www.nasa.gov), is the best way to find accurate information about natural disasters, such as hurricanes.

NOAA website, "The eye is a roughly circular area of comparatively light winds and fair weather found at the center of a severe tropical cyclone."

The time period when hurricanes occur most frequently is known as hurricane season. It occurs at different times in different places, which makes it important to know whether or not families live in a hurricane evacuation zone. This knowledge will help everyone better prepare for hurricanes and potential flooding from such disasters. Holding occasional evacuation drills ensures each member knows what to do and where to go when a hurricane strikes. Older students can practice helping with younger siblings and providing other assistance to help a family leave home quickly and easily.

Depending on the timing, a family may have to leave before a hurricane lands. Be prepared to leave before conditions worsen. If not ordered to leave, find a safe place to hunker down, away from windows and doors. As with other natural disasters, evacuation orders are designed to save lives. Obeying them is an essential safety measure.

Depending on a hurricane's strength, damage may be mild, moderate, or severe. Power may be out if the storm affected electricity lines or power grids. Using candles is a safe way to cope during the aftermath, but they should be handled carefully and be watched and extinguished properly. Students can help relatives and neighbors with cleanup, or they can team up to provide other assistance to help people cope with the aftermath of a hurricane.

Floods Up Close

Tropical storms dump excessive rain and cause flooding—the most common and widespread type of natural disaster. A flood happens when storm drains, the ground, and other infrastructure can no longer hold excess water. This can happen quickly, creating flash floods. Flash floods often occur with little notice or time to prepare, dumping large amounts of water. Coastal flooding, meanwhile, is often sparked by hurricanes. They, in turn, can cause storm surges that flood cities along the coast.

Depending on the amount of flooding, people can generally stay in their homes or businesses. When this isn't possible, they may have to evacuate. Sandbag walls are often used to protect homes and

Protecting property from flooding due to torrential rains and overflowing rivers may entail using sandbags, such as the ones around this McDonald's restaurant in Missouri.

buildings from flooding. For example, when flooding is expected, community resource organizations may provide sandbags to residents, coordinating time for residents to pick those up at no cost. Sandbags can help prevent or alleviate some of the flooding.

As with other extreme weather conditions, tune in to news reports for the most current information about current conditions. Listen for flood watches and warnings and flash flood watches and warnings. The watches alert that a flood is possible, while the warning means it is already underway or will shortly affect a community.

During a flood, try to move to a higher elevation within a home, building, or outdoor location. Don't walk or ride in a car through standing water. In the aftermath of a flood, avoid the temptation to help with cleanup. Standing water from a flood can be deadly because of the disease-causing bacteria that is attached to floating debris and garbage found in the water. Toys and games that were submerged in floodwaters should be tossed for the same reason.

Helping Pets

Pets are important members of families and can be affected by natural disasters, such as tropical storms and related flooding. Unfortunately, pets are often overlooked as people rush to find shelter or get help from first responders. Below are some ways to help pets during natural disasters:

- Include pet food and supplies in emergency response kits. Keep photos of your pets handy, as they might help to identity and locate a pet after a crisis.
- Let first responders know that there are pets inside the home or on the property. Let them know where they normally hang out for an easier rescue.
- Keep a list of pet-friendly shelters in the event of an evacuation. In some cases, families may not be able to choose which facility they go to, but when possible, the list will help them make pet-friendly choices.
- Never return to a flooded structure to retrieve a pet, as doing so can place people at risk for long-term injury or death.
- Get medical care for injured pets.

If a pet experiences new or renewed anxiety, consider taking it to a veterinarian. In some instances, veterinarians and shelters with veterinary staff may be willing to see animals at no cost or at reduced rates after a natural disaster.

CHAPTER FOUR

Snow Daze

A fierce February 2010 blizzard will long be remembered in the eastern parts of the United States. Nicknamed Snowmageddon, the storm dumped an astonishing amount of snow in a very short time. It blanketed the metro area of Maryland, Virginia, and Washington, DC. It became the fourth largest snowstorm in Washington, DC, totaling 17.8 inches (45 cm).

Other affected areas were hit harder. Some had snow totals reaching 20 inches (50 cm), and Virginia's Dulles Airport reported a whopping 34.5 inches (87 cm)! According to a *Washington Post* article, early estimates were that five hundred thousand tons of snow fell in Virginia.

Throughout the region, activity ground to a stop. Businesses, schools, and airports closed. Trains and buses stopped running. Trees and power lines toppled. Buildings and homes suffered roof damage because of the weight of the snow. Roads were impassable, and local, state, and federal government offices were forced to close for days.

New York City residents brave the outdoors following a February 2010 storm that dumped large amounts of snow in eastern parts of the United States.

Blizzard Basics

Snowmageddon illustrates the tremendous impact a blizzard has on people, property, and governments. Generally, a blizzard is a severe snowstorm. It is dangerous and distinguishes itself from other storms by:

- Strong winds—Wind speeds are greater than 35 mph (56 kmh) during a blizzard.
- Dense snow—Thick, blowing snow reduces visibility to less than a quarter mile or 440 yards (402 meters).
- Duration—It snows for more than three hours.

Some blizzards form from new snowfall, while others form as wind whips around previously fallen snow. In either case, a blizzard is dangerous. Many snowstorms may seem like blizzards because of the amount of snow that's dumped. But unless the storm has the three elements, it is not a blizzard. Compared to other snow events, blizzards are always more dangerous. It's tough to walk or drive during a blizzard because of these conditions, making outdoor activities dangerous. When walking, it's difficult to see people or cars coming in one's direction. When driving, it's difficult to see the road and other vehicles.

On Its Way

As blizzards form, meteorologists track their paths using radar and satellite technology. A blizzard warning is issued when they are certain the storm is forming and will hit a specific region. In many cases, schools and businesses will close in anticipation of the storm. After-school activities also are often cancelled to assure students are not stuck in a storm. The goal is to keep people safe, warm, and indoors.

Being inside is the best place to be during a blizzard. Going outside risks the possibility of being trapped or hurt in a blizzard. Because of the frigid air during a blizzard, the possibility of other medical problems, like frostbite, is high. Tune in to weather reports for up-to-date conditions, and only go outside when it's safe to do so.

Snow Safety

Snow looks so inviting when it falls, and many people accept the invitation to participate in snow-related activities. Building snow characters, playing with snowball fights, skiing, and sledding are popular ways to enjoy the white stuff before it melts and disappears. The key is to play safely. Wear warm, protective clothing and team up with others as often as possible in case you need each other during an emergency situation. If sledding, avoid riding on snow mounds that lead into roadways to avoid being hit by a vehicle. When skiing, use snowshoes that fit and equipment that matches your skill level.

Avalanches occur unexpectedly and quickly, as these athletes discovered while training in the Ukraine on Manyavsky, a frozen waterfall.

About Avalanches

Snow is beautiful, but it can be dangerous. An avalanche is a particularly dangerous snow event that can occur in snow-prone places like Antarctica as well as snowy ski resorts. Such places offer opportunities for snow enthusiasts to ski during the fall and winter. Some of the snow is natural, while other places use machines that manufacture snow, especially if there has not been significant snowfall in a given time.

When people ski or travel, they can shift snow. That shift moves the powder in expected ways. For example, if a skier is traveling downhill, the person's equipment will naturally move snow aside as he or she glides along designated paths.

Sometimes, unexpectedly, the snow shifts and moves rapidly. When that happens, the snow cascades down mountains or hills at an abnormally high speed, causing an avalanche. An avalanche can harm structures, towns, and people. Buildings, homes, and other structures are damaged when the snow leaves its normal resting places and tumbles into areas where people live and work.

Some avalanches are caused by the natural movement of the snow. Others are caused by activity on the snow, such as people using skis or snowmobiles. At times, however, an avalanche occurs when people are involved in unsafe activities on the snow. For example, people may ski in areas where such activity is prohibited. Doing so can cause an avalanche.

During an avalanche, people are hurt when the snow slams into them. They might break a bone or die because of the force of the snow during an avalanche or from being buried under it. When people are buried under snow, they must be rescued quickly in order to survive. Search and rescue teams have to work against the clock to save them. They use special equipment and search dogs to do so. Their job is easier if the trapped person is carrying a beeper that alerts rescuers to the person's position. When that's not the case, trained dogs assist in rescue efforts. It's a race against time because oxygen generally lasts for only twenty minutes. If a person is not rescued in that time, he or she will die.

Prepared for Snow

Blizzards and avalanches are natural disasters. Here are some ways to cope with them:

- Know before you go—Check the weather before going out to play in snow. Wait until a blizzard is over before going out to play or helping to shovel snow.
- Shine brightly—Wear brightly colored clothing. It stands out, making it easier for people to be seen—and found—in the event they're trapped in snow.
- Play safely—Use proper equipment and stay in areas designated as safe to play in.
- Do your school work—School may be out, but keeping up with scheduled assignments helps keep minds off of the snow. It also allows for an easier transition back into classwork once school resumes.
- Team up—Never go out on ski trails alone or at times when it is unsafe.
- Have ID available—It's a good idea to always have a school ID or some other identification

card. Doing so makes it easier for people to help students reconnect with their school or family.

Coping in the Aftermath

Snow happens. How people and communities respond will depend on whether they are prepared for pending weather and its aftermath. Students are

Playing in snow offers entertainment in the aftermath of a natural disaster, but always carry ID so that you can easily be reconnected with friends and family.

not immune to these natural disasters. They can get caught in storms at home, while traveling on school trips, or while on vacation with relatives. Some ways to cope in the aftermath of a snow event include the following:

- Follow safety instructions—Sometimes blizzards happen while people are at school,

If you are having trouble coping with the aftermath of a natural disaster, speak with a trusted adult to get help and relief.

at a mall, in a dance studio, or volunteering at a shelter. If that occurs, follow the safety instructions from those in charge.

- Get immediate help—If you are separated from family and friends, call 911 to report your location and what happened.
- Be cooperative—Emergencies can bring out the worst in people, especially when they are worried about themselves or others. Try and be cooperative during a snow event.
- Help others—In the aftermath of a blizzard, some neighbors—especially elderly individuals or those with disabilities—will need help with snow removal. Whether students volunteer or charge a fee, they become essential community helpers by clearing sidewalks and driveways of snow as quickly as possible.
- Get long-term help—Natural disasters cause all kinds of emotional and mental distress. In the aftermath of a blizzard or avalanche, speak with a parent, guardian, guidance counselor, or other trusted adult about recurring nightmares, stress, or other problems. It is possible that counseling from a mental health professional may be needed. Combined help can pave the way for students to overcome fear, depression, insomnia, or other trauma-related conditions.

10 Great Questions to Ask a Storm Chaser

1. How did you become fascinated with storms?
2. What made you want to chase storms?
3. What qualities do you think make a good storm chaser?
4. What special training did you have to receive to get a job in your field?
5. What special equipment do you use when chasing storms?
6. If you ever experience fear, how do you still do your job?
7. What is the best part of your job?
8. What is the biggest storm you ever chased?
9. How is your job different from an on-air meteorologist?
10. What subjects do you suggest students study if interested in becoming a storm chaser?

CHAPTER FIVE

Shake, Rattle, Spin

"*Did you feel that?*" This question is asked a lot when the world seems to suddenly tilt and then correct itself. People ask relatives, friends, coworkers, and even strangers if and when they felt a tremor, shake, or similar ground movement. On social media, people post the same question to friends and followers. They wonder if they imagined the sensation—or if it was an earthquake.

Without doubt, when an earthquake is major, there is no question. The destruction is visible, and there may be foreshocks or aftershocks. People may be hurt or even killed. In Indonesia, more than 1,200 people died from a 7.5 magnitude earthquake and the tsunami it spurred on September 28, 2018.

As Earth Moves

Earthquakes happen because Earth is a planet of rock. That rock forms Earth's sections or layers: crust (top),

In August 2018, Lombok Island in Indonesia experienced a powerful 7.0 magnitude earthquake that rocked villages, causing permanent damage to numerous structures.

core (center), and mantle (middle). Earth's crust ranges "from about 10 to 65 km in thickness worldwide," according to the online "Earthquake Glossary" on the US Geological Survey (USGS) website. A science-focused government agency, the USGS records and reports earthquakes as part of its research involving the United States and its natural resources.

The crust is not one solid piece of rock, but rather many blocks that scientists call tectonic plates. Those plates are what contribute to earthquakes. Generally, Earth is always moving, but the pace is so incredibly slow that people can't feel the shifts. At times, however, the tectonic plates slip past each other, causing an earthquake.

Earthquakes have occurred for centuries. They happen all around the world, with multiple ones occurring *each day*. In the United States, for example, California is prone to earthquakes because it sits on the San Andreas Fault Zone, an area caused by a tectonic shift millions of years ago.

Size Matters

Unlike some weather conditions, such as hurricanes, earthquakes cannot be predicted. But they can be understood and measured. On its "About Us—Program Overview," the USGS notes that its earthquake-related work is crucial in helping citizens, emergency responders, and engineers understand key elements of each earthquake.

Scientists who study earthquakes are called seismologists. They use two measuring tools—the Richter and the Modified Mercalli intensity scales. The Richter measures an earthquake's strength or magnitude from 1–10. The Modified Mercalli measures the intensity of damage, ranging from I to X. On each, the higher the number, the worse the strength or damage.

The largest-ever earthquake occurred on May 22, 1960, in the city of Valdivia in southern Chile. It measured 9.5 on the Richter scale. The largest earthquake in the United States occurred on March 27, 1964, not far from Anchorage, Alaska. It was a 9.2-magnitude earthquake and remains the largest

Tectonic plates

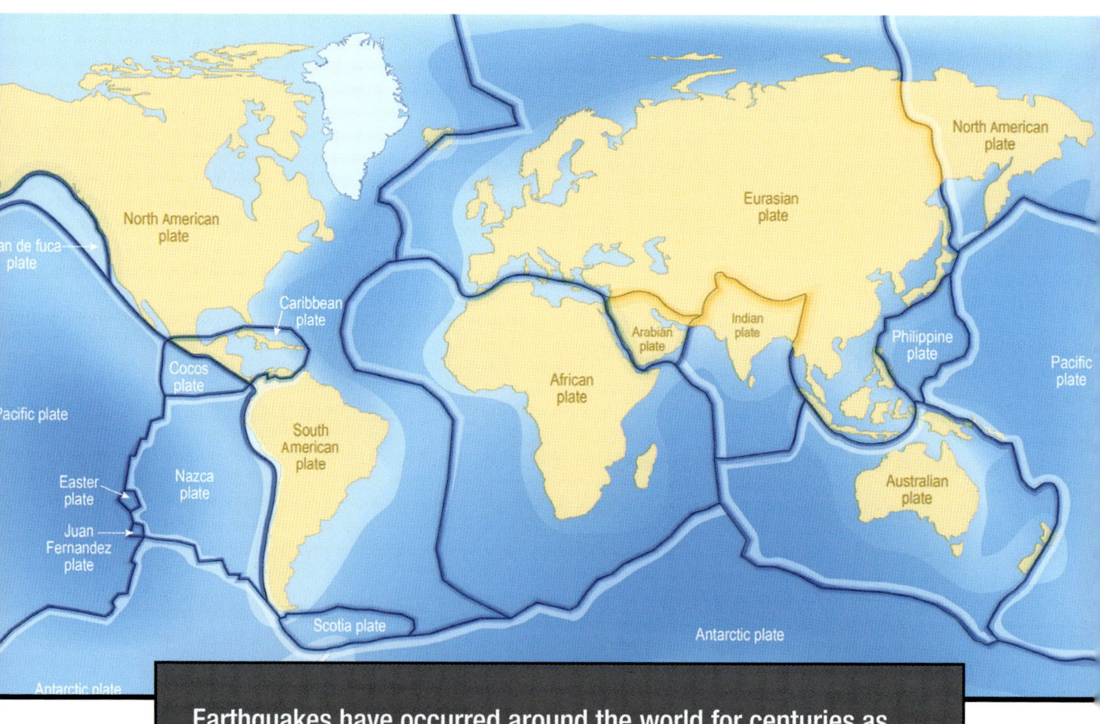

Earthquakes have occurred around the world for centuries as a result of the movement of the planet's tectonic plates. Their degrees of intensity range from mild to permanently destructive.

ever after the Valdivia event. According to Natural Resources Canada, Canada experiences more than four thousand small earthquakes each year. The worst one in Canada happened centuries ago. On January 26, 1700, it measured 9.0 and occurred in the Cascadia Subduction Zone near British Columbia.

Safety Measures

Because of the unpredictable nature of earthquakes, effective safety precautions are essential. In areas where earthquakes frequently occur, building codes are established to ensure structures can withstand the effect. Older buildings that were designed prior to such codes are often required to make major structural changes so they, too, can withstand earthquakes.

In earthquake-prone areas, schools conduct drills to foster earthquake awareness and teach safety. They help students know what to do, where to go, and how to act if the ground suddenly starts shaking. Away from schools, students can encourage such drills with their families.

During an earthquake, find a safe place to wait it out. Also, stay clear of furniture, TVs, and other large items that have the potential to fall and injure someone. Avoid windows because they can break and shatter into millions of pieces, causing injuries.

After an Earthquake

Ways to cope with the aftermath of an earthquake vary, depending on how severe it is. In a mild earthquake, for example, many people are able to resume their daily activities, like finishing out a school day. More severe earthquakes can damage buildings, roads, and other structures.

Don't Answer That!

An earthquake is shocking. As with other emergencies, people want to share their stories. Calling a relative, friend, or classmate is natural, but that may not be the wisest thing to do as it can contribute to blocked telephone lines.

What's the big deal? Emergency workers rely on phone lines to share information among themselves and answer and respond to residents' calls for help. The more people chatting on landlines or cell phones, the harder it can be for emergency calls to get through. Instead of making a phone call, send a text. Share your whereabouts and well-being with loved ones, and offer to make calls once everything calms down.

In these instances, students should follow safety procedures.

Expect things to be different outside and maybe even unsafe. An earthquake can cause windows to break and fall from buildings. Other parts of the building may tumble if damages occurred. Staying away from the structures reduces the risk of being hurt.

How soon it's safe to go back indoors depends on the damage. Be careful if you go back inside. Things may be knocked down, and glass and other materials may be scattered on the floor. Items in cabinets may also have shifted, posing a safety hazard.

Terrible Twisters

Like hurricanes, tornadoes can cause mass destruction. A tornado is an extreme and violent storm occurring on land or on water like a "waterspout." In fact, the NOAA classifies it as "the most violent of all atmospheric storms" in an article on its website. It basically is spinning air that connects a storm cloud to the ground, according to meteorologist and TV host Al Roker in his book *Al Roker's Extreme Weather: Tornadoes, Typhoons, and Other Weather Phenomena.*

Dark skies, rain or hail, and an eerie quietness are signs that a tornado is coming. A tornado

A record number of tornadoes—more than 225—occured in the United States over twelve days in May 2019.

appears as a funnel-shaped cloud. Because of its twisting nature, many people nickname them twisters. Like other natural disasters, tornadoes occur throughout the world. They really are dangerous storms. In the United States, they happen most frequently in the central states. That's why the region is nicknamed Tornado Alley. However, other areas are slammed. Each year, about 1,200 tornadoes touch down and wreak havoc.

Because of their frequency, tornadoes are viewed in terms of the seasons or times of the year in which they occur.

Most tornadoes appear in the spring and early summer, but don't be fooled, as a tornado can happen anytime if prime conditions are in place.

How Strong Is It?

Wind is a key component of a tornado. Its speed determines how severe the storm is. The National Weather Service determines the speed by looking

Hail's Fury

Hail is dangerous. Unfortunately, many people underestimate it. They think it's just small, pebble-sized pieces of ice. On the contrary, some hail is the size of golf balls. Large bits like these can severely damage windshields and become a driving hazard.

Don't underestimate the size or fury of hail. Be careful while walking outside, and take cover to avoid injury. Also, remember hail is hard. Throwing it at friends like a snowball can hurt them. Don't do it. Above all, seek cover *inside* if it's hailing.

at how much damage has occurred to such things as buildings and trees. They use a measuring device called the Enhanced Fujita (EF) scale to access the wind speed. The scale's measurements range from EF0 to EF5. Measured wind speeds range from 65–200 mph (105–322 kmh)!

The worst tornadoes form rotating thunderstorms. These so-called supercells are

Hail is small yet powerful and has the potential to shatter windows, crack car windshields, and hurt people upon contact.

very destructive. They pose major risks to people, property, and the environment. Such a tornado can flatten a house, like in the movie *The Wizard of Oz*. It can toss cars and mobile homes around and uproot trees. Some tornadoes also bring hail!

Safe and Sound

Staying out of the path of any tornado is the key to surviving it. When there is a risk of a tornado, either a tornado watch or tornado warning is issued. The watch basically alerts residents to the risk of a tornado, meaning that it might occur in an area or nearby. However, a warning means that a tornado will definitely hit—and soon!

Many schools have designated places, such as a gymnasium, for students to go to at such times. Other times, students will "shelter in place," meaning they stay where they are and take cover as best they can. These locations can include classrooms, cafeterias, libraries, and gymnasiums.

In tornado-prone areas, many homes have underground storm cellars where people can wait out the storm. For homes without such protection, the best place to hide is in the lowest floor of a home or building, often the basement. Hiding in a closet or bathtub are also ways to stay safe.

Sometimes, though, a tornado strikes while people are outside. If that happens, try to get to a safe structure. That may mean running into a nearby store or mall. When riding in a car, the best place to hide is in a nearby ditch if one is close by. Community storm shelters are other safe havens.

When a tornado struck in Utica, Illinois, the resident pictured hid in a basement, which protected him from the powerful forces that destroyed the home.

After the Twister

Some tornadoes pass through quickly, while others take their sweet time. Some, for example, last only a few seconds, while others can last a full hour. But there is no guarantee. Never leave a place of safety before being absolutely sure that the tornado is no longer in the immediate area. In the aftermath, check in with relatives. Once outside, stay away from any downed power lines or trees and damaged structures.

CHAPTER SIX

Forest on Fire

Gender-reveal parties are popular with parents who want to share the gender of their unborn child. For one father-to-be in Tucson, Arizona, it was also costly. He was off duty from his job as a Border Patrol agent and enjoying the celebration on April 23, 2017. It was a hot day on which the National Weather Service had issued a "fire watch," which signals perfect conditions for fire.

He excitedly shot off a target filled with a colored powder and a legal explosive. Unfortunately, it sparked a wildfire. The "Sawmill Fire" raged for more than a week. About 800 firefighters battled the wildfire, which impacted more than 47,000 acres (19,020 hectares), according to Curt Prendergast's article in the *Arizona Daily Star*.

The "Sawmill Fire" burns through the night. Started accidently, it burned thousands of acres of land in Arizona and lasted for more than a week.

The dad-to-be admitted it was his fault and was charged for his role. The original amount he agreed to pay was $8 million, according to Eric Mack's article on Forbes.com. That amount was reduced to $220,000 by a judge. He also received a five-year-probation sentence. His action is an example of how people can start wildfires.

Fire Facts

Fire is useful, powerful, and destructive. From heating homes to cooking meals and even preventing fires in the wild, it is essential for everyday life. But its destructive nature is legendary. Fire has leveled homes, burned through forests, and even melted heavy equipment and cars. The devastation has caused billions of dollars in

Three elements must be present to start a fire: fuel, oxygen, and heat. This is known as the "fire triangle." Remove one of the elements, and the fire will extinguish.

damage. Thousands of people have been injured and many have been killed.

Fire occurs when three factors exist: heat, fuel, and oxygen. This is commonly called "the fire triangle." All three must exist for a fire to start. A fire's intensity, location, and other factors determine its impact.

The source of heat can vary. It is what starts—or ignites—the fire. Heat is also needed for the fire to continue to burn. Some heat sources include flame from a match, fireworks, or similar item. Weather conditions such as lightning also can start a fire. Fuel is anything that can be burned. It can be wood, dried brush in a forest, clothing, furniture, and many other things. Items containing chemicals also catch fire. The third part of the fire triangle is oxygen. It is in the air, making it easy for a fire to ignite.

The key to extinguishing a fire is to quickly remove one of the parts of the triangle. Sometimes a fire may just die out because the fuel, heat, or oxygen is eliminated. If that does not happen, a fire will need to be extinguished through normal fire protection measures. For example, a fire extinguisher may be used to stop a fire in a home. (Using a fire extinguisher correctly is important to minimize damage and avoid injury.)

Calling for help is often required. In a community, paid or volunteer firefighters will

Fire Fascination

Some people find fire fascinating, so they pursue fire-related careers. Others don't handle their interest in a positive way. They set fires, such as the "Holy Fire" in the Holy Jim Canyon area of the

The "Holy Fire" lights up the California sky as stunned residents look from a distance. The fire was caused by arson and burned thousands of acres.

Cleveland National Park in California. It was set on August 6, 2018, affected 23,000 acres (9,307 ha), and lasted more than a month. Purposefully setting fires is a crime called arson. The arsonist was arrested.

How should someone handle fascination with fire? If it's negative, seek help from mental health professionals *before* setting fires and harming property or people. If it's positive, talk with a guidance counselor about viable fire-related careers.

team up to battle blazes. For a large-scale event, neighboring fire departments may need to assist. Fire is classified in terms of "alarms." Each escalating alarm indicates the need for additional fire personnel. A one-alarm fire, for example, means only one team—or company—is needed to tackle the conditions. A two-alarm fire means an additional company is needed to help and so on.

About Wildfires

A wildfire is a fire occurring in a forest or grassland. Every year, more than one hundred thousand wildfires occur throughout the United States and burn millions of acres. Some wildfires happen naturally. Others are sparked by extreme heat, drought, or other weather conditions.

In a dense forest, the extensive number of trees can cause fire to easily spread as it moves from one tree to another. The intense heat is dangerous to fight and difficult to put out. It is hard to imagine how hot they get. Some can reach up to 2,000 degrees Fahrenheit (1,100 degrees Celsius)! On average, they spread about 12 mph (20 kmh) but can spread more rapidly under the right conditions.

People also cause wildfires, often accidentally. Sometimes it is because a cigarette or campfire was not properly extinguished. Other times, it's because lit fireworks unexpectedly hit something, bursting into flames. Ignoring burn bans also spurs fires. A burn ban is designed to protect areas where fires start easily and cause extensive damage. The ban prohibits people from burning trash, using matches, or starting campfires. Ignoring this is not just unwise; it's dangerous. Once fires start in these fragile areas, they cause extensive harm. Never, ever ignore a burn ban.

Types of Wildfires

There are different types of wildfires. They are typed by the fuel involved. For example, a brush fire feeds on grass, branches, and other things on the ground.

Crown fires are those burning in the tops of trees, a phenomenon that happens during large fires.

A firestorm is the most dangerous and biggest fire. These destructive forces can create windy conditions, further fueling fire as embers carried by wind land and spark fires at other locations. And the smoke can rise hundreds or thousands of feet into the air, causing hazardous breathing conditions. All types pose problems for wildlife. When the fire is intense or large, animals may not have a chance to escape. In such cases, many are killed.

Tools of the Trade

Fighting wildfires is a complicated process. Wildfires require special equipment and personnel because there are no available hydrants to pump needed water. Water must be brought in. Airplanes filled with it fly over the affected area, dumping water. These "water bombers" are especially important in areas where firefighters are prevented from getting close because of intense heat or flames.

Firefighters, dubbed "smoke jumpers," tackle fires in remote areas that are hard to reach by land. They are flown over affected areas and use parachutes to land in a safe place. Their equipment is also released. Technology, such as satellites, is used to track fires and identify outbreaks.

Some fires are fought from the ground with assistance from air tanks that spray water over difficult-to-reach areas.

Sometimes it is necessary to fight fire with fire. This is called a prescribed burn, and it is a preventative measure. Sometimes fire is set in very dry areas or where a wildfire has not happened in a long time to prevent brush fires. They are set because there is a high risk of a fire. Setting one can reduce worse events. It is strictly controlled.

The goal is to prevent the fire from spreading beyond the control area, usually located far away from property or people. On the surface, it is a good idea but also is a controversial practice. As with other fires, a prescribed burn can get out of hand, resulting in damage that would not have otherwise occurred.

Wildfire Safety

As with other natural disasters, prevention is important. Be careful to extinguish matches fully—and of course, don't play with them, ever. After camping with family or friends, make sure someone is assigned to check that it's out and cooled before leaving the campsite. FEMA also suggests creating a "fire resistant zone." On its READY.gov article about wildfires, FEMA explains that such a zone is an area "free of leaves, debris or flammable materials for at least 30 feet [9 m] from your home." Work with a trusted adult to create one.

Sometimes a fire spreads far beyond its origin, closing in on towns and other populated areas. Staying safe requires being vigilant. Tune in to news reports for alerts and updates, and be prepared to leave an affected area as quickly as possible. When the risk is high, evacuation may be voluntary or mandatory. Obeying an evacuation order increases the chance of survival. In the aftermath of a wildfire, focus on staying safe. It is important to avoid an area until it has been deemed OK to return. Expect the unexpected. Be prepared for lingering sights and smells. Even if a home is spared, there may be gutted neighboring homes or businesses. Sometimes homes have smoke damage, making it impossible to be used until they air out. If needed, wear a mask to prevent inhaling smoke.

A community affected by fire will not look the same. Be prepared to experience myriad emotions while walking through familiar areas.

When returning home, beware of burned items. They may be hot enough to cause injury. Often, people have to do various tasks to deal with the aftermath of a wildfire. If needed for insurance purposes, help take photos of damaged belongings or property. Volunteering to help with cleanup or other safe restoration activities can help students recover in the aftermath of a wildfire. But, sometimes, the aftermath of a wildfire is filled with angst. So much is lost or damaged, much of which can never be replaced. If feeling overwhelmed, share feelings and concerns with relatives or other trusted adults. If needed, get help from a mental health professional.

CHAPTER SEVEN

Brighter Forecast

Natural disasters occur for different reasons. Some are sparked by extreme weather. Some are haphazardly triggered by people's actions. Some can be identified and tracked before they strike, while others arise unexpectedly and quickly. The devastation is often far-reaching. Students will be affected—or they will know someone who is.

In a natural disaster, adrenaline may help people quickly respond and get out of harm's way. As the emergency passes, negative feelings can replace positive energy. In the aftermath of a natural disaster, students should expect myriad feelings. Those will vary based on what was seen and experienced. Sadness, depression, anger, and fear are common feelings and conditions.

Some students also may struggle with "survivor's guilt." That's a condition where people

Coping in the aftermath of a natural disaster can be troubling, but it is not impossible. Friends, family members, professional therapists, and community resources can help.

feel guilty because they were not harmed or killed but someone else was. Sometimes a person with survivor's guilt feels completely empty—or numb. Really, there are many different emotions a person may experience. That is to be expected.

About PTSD

A natural disaster is a high-stress event. After one, people may have lingering long-term stress and related ailments. This is called post-traumatic stress disorder (PTSD). PTSD affects people of all ages. It affects them emotionally and mentally and sometimes physically. Because of the condition, a person may not be able to resume regular activities, such as going to school or work.

PTSD is not an imaginary condition. It is debilitating and won't go away on its own. Rather, it is a medical condition that requires a doctor's diagnosis and treatment. Help is available. Medications, or even a service or support animal, can help alleviate some of the symptoms.

Disabilities and Natural Disasters

In the aftermath of a disaster, relatives or neighbors may need help because of visible and unseen disabilities. Wherever possible, try and assist—or let rescuers know about someone who may have

Residents with disabilities may need extra help getting basic needs to survive a natural disaster. In the photo below, the National Guard stepped in to provide food and water.

difficulty leaving an area because of a physical disability.

Students with disabilities need help just like their neighbors. After an earthquake, for example, elevators may not be accessible. If rescuers know a student has a low-vision disability, they will make sure someone partners with the student to carefully help him or her down stairs and out of the building.

Some considerations for students with disabilities are as follows:

- Be prepared. Have all medications in one place, such as the family's disaster kit. Make sure a student's items are clearly labeled. Include information about medical devices so that rescuers or helpers can successfully assist a student with a disability.

- Keep disability aids close by so that they will not be overlooked and forgotten.
- Carry ID and emergency contact information available for sharing in the event a disability prevents verbally communicating information to first responders.
- Use a medical bracelet or similar device to help people be aware of unseen conditions, such as allergies or medical conditions like diabetes.
- Remember service animal needs. Have a kit just for it with enough water, food, blankets, and other items needed in an emergency.
- Host drills to help students with disabilities know what to do in an emergency and how to best accommodate special needs. Students should know the plan, which friend or relative is assigned to help them, and whom to contact if separated from family.

Coping Strategies

Natural disasters are devastating. The following are some effective ways for coping in the aftermath of a natural disaster:

Reliable Information

It is impossible to thrive after a natural disaster without reliable information. Be proactive in getting and sharing information. Choose your preferred medium—such as TV, radio, or internet—and make sure it's providing current information, including alerts, warnings, and local weather conditions. Also, check out social media accounts for reputable, local and national meteorologists, TV stations, and newspapers. Like those pages and turn your notifications on so you know when updates are posted.

Personal Documents

It's important to have a safe place for storing birth certificates, school records, insurance policies, and other identifying paperwork in case they're needed. It's also essential to have a copy somewhere else other than at home in case an apartment or house is damaged or destroyed. Parents and guardians may choose to use bank safe deposit boxes or give copies of important documents to trusted relatives.

Emergency Contacts

In an emergency, it is important for first responders, school administrators, and medical personnel to know whom to contact if a student is injured in a natural disaster. Most schools require emergency contacts be updated each year. It's important to fulfill this requirement so that relatives can be immediately notified.

Purposeful Self-Care

The first thing on people's mind when a disaster strikes is usually themselves. They want to survive the ordeal. (A close second priority is the well-being of loved ones.) However, in the aftermath of an event, people sometimes forget to take good care of themselves because they are busy trying to deal with all of the issues arising from a natural disaster. But it's really important to practice purposeful self-care. Students do that when they do any or all of the following:

- Express thoughts and feelings—Sure, everybody may be busy dealing with their own feelings, but it's important to talk about those students are dealing with. Fear, frustration, extreme sadness, confusion—all of those feelings are valid in such circumstances. Don't bury or hide them. Talk about them so others can help you deal with these complex trauma-related emotions. Talk with family members, a spiritual leader, a guidance counselor, or a mental health professional.

- Tune out—In the aftermath of a natural disaster, it seems impossible to turn away from graphic images and information regarding various aspects of the events. Sometimes, it's too much to process and it can spark anxiety and other feelings. Know it's OK to tune out. Take a break from watching or reading the news. Ignore social media posts—or even take a

A break from ongoing news reports can be emotionally refreshing in the aftermath of a natural disaster. Consider spending time with friends and taking part in stress-free fun.

temporary social media break. Don't get drawn into conversations about what's happening. Instead, let others know the constant barrage of information is overwhelming so a break is needed. Invite them to share only urgent information.

- Stay connected—After a disaster, sometimes people want to be alone. While withdrawing may seem the easiest option to avoid tough questions or because one's not feeling great, isolation only complicates matters. Temporarily withdrawing from others usually is not an issue. However, long-term isolation breeds discouragement, discontent, and hopelessness. So, stay connected. Join in family gatherings and celebrations. Connect in person via phone or online with classmates and other friends. Consider returning to fun activities that you enjoyed prior to the disaster.
- Eat up—Food fuels bodies, providing needed strength to handle ordinary and extraordinary tasks and responsibilities. In the aftermath of a natural disaster, physical health is as important as mental and emotional well-being. So, try and eat. Encourage other family members to eat also.

Make it fun by cooking together, making yummy treats that usually are hard to resist. If you're having difficulty, get help. Talk with a counselor, trusted adult, or physician to determine how you can regain your appetite and resume eating for optimal health.

- Avoid self-harm—Some people resort to self-harm when they can't cope with trauma-

Cooking your favorite dish with a friend can be fun, relaxing, and a good reminder to eat healthy foods in the wake of a natural disaster.

filled situations like natural disasters. Some will drink alcohol, take illegal drugs, cut themselves, or engage in destructive behavior. Such behavior can never bring back what was lost or damaged in a natural disaster. Indeed, hurting oneself is never the best way to deal with life's tough issues and circumstances. In fact, it can make a bad situation worse. That's why students considering harming themselves should seek immediate help—as soon as possible!

- Seek counseling—Counseling services are often readily available in the aftermath of a natural disaster. Schools and other community relief organizations provide counseling. Going to one of those or seeing one's regular therapist may be useful. In-person counseling is one option, but counseling can also be done via telephone. The Suicide Hotline at (800) 273-8255, for example, is available twenty-four hours a day.
- Help others—Sometimes taking the focus off one's problems by helping others is an effective way to cope. Helping others is a great way to give back to the community or earn community service hours, even if a student is not directly impacted by an event. Help feed

Scam Alert

One way to help during a natural disaster is to donate money to different organizations. Use caution, though, as crooks often attempt to scam people who have a genuine desire to help in emergencies. These scams include fund-raising schemes organized without victims' permission or knowledge. Avoid being scammed with these tips:

- Only donate to reputable organizations.
- Don't give financial information to strangers who call for donations.
- Get a receipt in case a charge needs to be disputed.
- Don't use a debit card, as it is directly linked to checking accounts.

If scammed, contact a bank or credit card company to report the incident. Also let local law enforcement know what happened.

the homeless or disaster victims. Volunteer to clean up debris, shovel snow, or provide additional assistance. Consider babysitting young children so their parents are free to handle disaster-related challenges.

Focus on the Future

Knowledge is power, and knowing about natural disasters can help alleviate anxieties based about myths or misinformation. The more you know about a natural disaster, the better prepared you can be. Preparation is key.

Coping in the aftermath of a natural disaster sometimes entails using community resources to help with immediate needs. Individuals, families, business owners, and others receive help for everyday and emergency needs. Churches and other religious organizations, nonprofits, and other community groups often team up to provide needed help. They want to help residents cope in the aftermath of a natural disaster. They do so by providing a variety of services, including food distribution, clothing "closets," and counseling.

Take advantage of those, as needed. Food banks are also essential resources in the aftermath of a natural disaster. They offer a variety of food for children and adults. Some also have food for

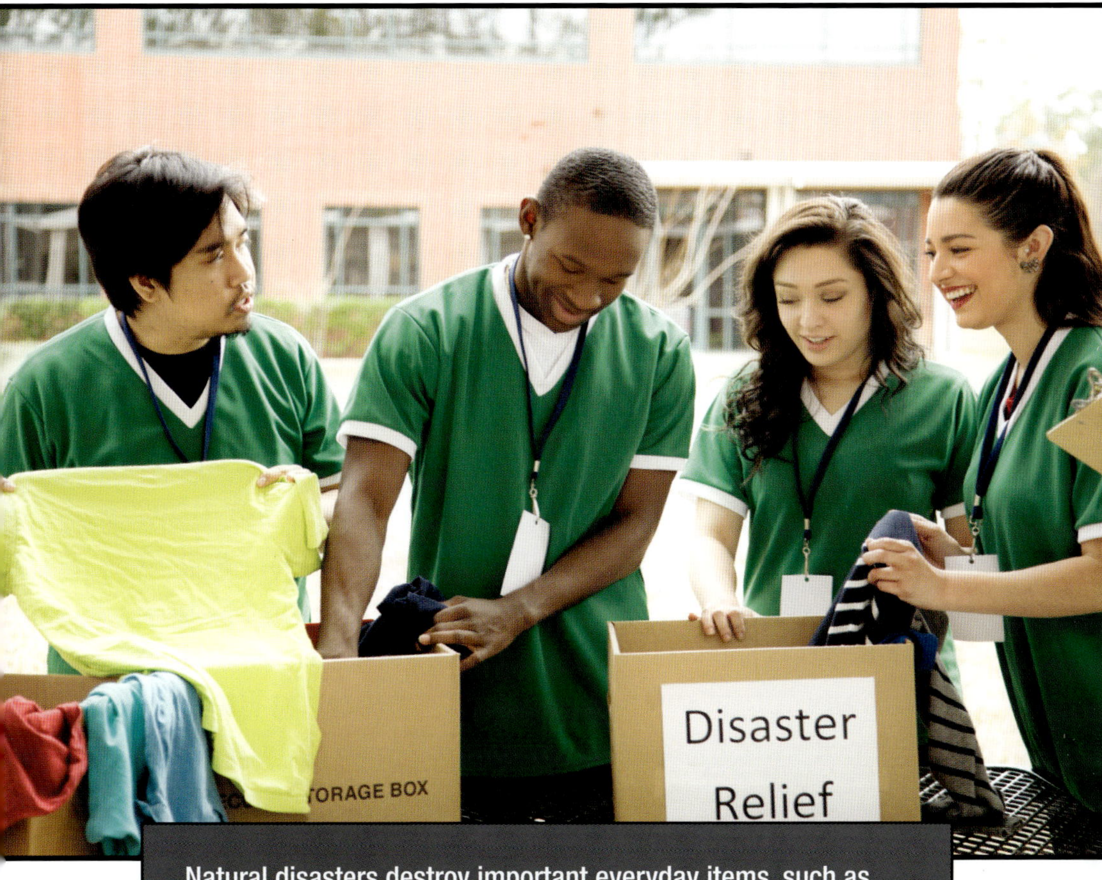

Natural disasters destroy important everyday items, such as shoes and apparel. A clothing drive can go a long way in helping others replace their belongings and feel supported.

infants. Also, use temporary shelters for emergency housing. Don't be afraid to go, as you will likely see other students and community members you already know.

Coping well does not mean burying one's head and acting like nothing happened. Rather, it means making the most of a bad situation and adjusting as well as possible to the new normal created from the aftermath of a natural disaster.

The adjustment period varies for each person, so it's important not to rush the grieving process. At the same time, if one's coping mechanism is just not kicking in, it's important to seek help. Trusted adults and mental health professionals can help students gather the courage and strength to be resilient.

Coping with the aftermath of a natural disaster is possible. Recovery can occur over time, and emotional well-being can be restored. Keep in mind, it does not happen overnight. Some things will never be exactly the same. While that may be disappointing or sad, it is worth noting so students do not unrealistically wait for things to be the same as they once were. Additionally, it is better to be armed with knowledge and know what to do than worrying about the "what if's"—some of which may never materialize!

The Road Ahead

Facing the challenges of a natural disaster begins with information and preparation. Keep in mind, natural disasters pose a challenge to the entire world. Remember, many strike without warning, and others do not conform to predictions. They may last longer, cause more damage, or harm more lives than expected. That's why knowing how to cope in the aftermath of a natural disaster is important.

When people cope well, they not only survive long-term, but they thrive. They embrace the courage and strength to resume their lives. They get help when needed with mental or emotional distress. They team up to help others, and they use community or government resources to rebuild. As a result, people are emotionally and mentally ready to face the future—even if that means facing yet another natural disaster.

Glossary

aftershock A smaller, less severe tremor that occurs after an earthquake.

burn ban A mandatory restriction imposed to prevent fires, including wildfires.

crust The outer layer of Earth.

curfew A mandatory restriction designed to keep people from being outdoors during emergencies, such as national disasters.

drought A long-term dry weather condition that develops in the absence of rainfall.

evacuation order An official declaration advising people that they must leave an area because of hazardous conditions caused by a natural disaster.

fire triangle Commonly refers to fuel, heat, and oxygen, the three elements needed to start and maintain a fire.

flash flood A fast-moving flood that occurs with short notice and dumps great quantities of rain.

foreshock A smaller earthquake that's felt before a larger earthquake occurs.

magnitude The strength or intensity of an earthquake; the higher the magnitude, the greater the earthquake and resulting damage.

meteorologist A scientist whose specialty is weather.

National Weather Service (NWS) A US agency that provides essential weather-related information, data, and services.

PTSD The acronym for post-traumatic stress disorder, a condition caused by trauma-filled situations, such as natural disasters.

Richter scale The measuring device meteorologists use to measure an earthquake's intensity.

sandbag wall A group of sandbags stacked together and placed around homes and buildings to prevent flooding.

scam A dishonest activity or operation designed to cheat people, businesses, or governments.

storm chaser An amateur or professional (like a meteorologist) who closely follows extreme weather, traveling to areas to get information, photos, or an experiential thrill.

supercell A rotating thunderstorm that forms a tornado.

tectonic plates Sections of Earth's crust that contribute to most earthquakes.

warning A notice issued when a natural disaster will definitely occur.

watch A notice issued about the possibility of a natural disaster.

For More Information

Environment Canada

Environment and Climate Change Canada

Meteorological Service of Canada

National Inquiry Response Team

351 St-Joseph Boulevard, Room 7034

Gatineau, QC K1A 0H3

Canada

Website: https://weather.gc.ca

Environment Canada and its partner agencies serve as a source for information about Canada's environment and natural resources, including current weather, public alerts, and scientific information about forecasts and other topics.

Federal Emergency Management Agency (FEMA)

500 C Street SW

Washington, DC 20472

(202) 646-2500

Website: http://www.fema.gov

Facebook: @FEMA

Twitter: @fema

YouTube: FEMA

FEMA offers podcasts and information about emergency preparedness, national disasters, its Youth Preparedness Council, and more.

Get Prepared Canada

Email: info@GetPrepared.ca

(800) O-CANADA (622-6232)

Website: https://www.getprepared.gc.ca/index-en.aspx

Twitter: @Get_Prepared

YouTube: Safety in Canada

Get Prepared offers Canadian government information and resources about emergency preparedness, including emergency kits and material for people with disabilities or special needs.

National Weather Service (NWS)

1325 East West Highway

Silver Spring, MD 20910

Website: https://www.weather.gov

Facebook and Twitter: @NWS

YouTube: usweathergov

The National Weather Service is a US federal government agency. Its website offers forecasts, active alerts, safety information, climate data, and more.

SciJinks
Jet Propulsion Laboratory
4800 Oak Grove Drive
M/S 201-101
Pasadena, CA 91109
Email: scijinks.info@noaa.gov.
Website: https://scijinks.gov
Facebook and Twitter: @ scijinks
YouTube: NOAA SciJinks

SciJinks, a website sponsored by the National Oceanographic and Atmospheric Administration (NOAA), offers games (including simulations), videos, career profiles, and other weather-related information for students in middle school and high school.

US Geological Survey (USGS)
12201 Sunrise Valley Drive
Reston, VA, 20192
(888) ASK-USGS (275-8747)
Website: https://earthquake.usgs.gov/learn/kids
Facebook: @USGeologicalSurvey
Twitter: @USGS
YouTube: USGS

The US Geological Survey's earthquake page for kids showcases animation videos, a "Today in Earthquake History" page, fact sheets, science project ideas, and links to activities.

US Global Change Research Program (USGCRP)
1800 G Street NW, Suite 9100
Washington, DC 20006
(202) 223-6262
Website: https://www.globalchange.gov/climate-change
Facebook: @usgcrp
Twitter: @usgcrp

The USGCRP conducts research to understand Earth's systems, including the atmosphere, ecosystems, ice, land, oceans, and human beings.

University Corporation for Atmospheric Research (UCAR)
1850 Table Mesa Drive
Boulder, CO 80301
(303) 497-1000
Email: scied@ucar.edu
Website: https://scied.ucar.edu/students
Facebook: @UCARscied
Instagram: @ucarscied
Twitter: @UCARSciEd
YouTube: UCARConnect

UCAR provides information, activities, and games about weather for students.

For Further Reading

Drimmer, Stephanie Warren. *National Geographic Kids Ultimate Weatherpedia: The Most Complete Weather Reference Ever.* Washington, DC: National Geographic Children's Books, 2019.

Kostigen, Thomas M. *Extreme Weather: Surviving Tornadoes, Sandstorms, Hailstorms, Blizzards, Hurricanes and More!* Washington, DC: National Geographic Society, 2014.

Lusted, Marcia Amidon, ed. *Extreme Weather Events* (Global Viewpoints). New York, NY: Greenhaven Press, 2017.

Machajewski, Sarah. *Weather and Climate Around the World* (Spotlight on Weather and Natural Disasters). New York, NY: PowerKids Press, 2019.

Malizia, Diana. *A Visual Guide to Weather and Climate* (Visual Exploration of Science). New York, NY: Rosen Young Adult, 2018.

Nagle, Jeanne. *The World's Most Tragic Disasters* (Making Headlines). New York, NY: Enslow Publishing, 2017.

Roker, Al. *Al Roker's Extreme Weather: Tornadoes, Typhoons, and Other Weather Phenomena.* New York, NY: HarperCollins Publishers, 2017.

Tarshis, Lauren. *I Survived True Stories. Five Epic Stories.* New York: NY: Scholastic Press, 2014.

Watts, Claire. *Eyewitness Natural Disasters.* New York, NY: DK Publishing, 2015.

Way, Jennifer L. *Severe-Storm Scientists: Chasing Tornadoes and Hurricanes* (Extreme Science Careers). New York, NY: Enslow Publishing, 2015.

Bibliography

City News Service and Jonathan Lloyd. "Holy Fire Flares Up in Cleveland Forest." NBC 7, August 27, 2018. https://www.nbcsandiego.com/news/local/Holy-Fire-Wildfire-California-Containment-Firefighters-491813691.html.

Cullinane, Susannah, and Joe Sterling. "5 Minutes of Warning, Then Tornadoes So Powerful They Killed 23 People in Alabama." CNN.com, March 4, 2019. https://www.cnn.com/2019/03/04/us/tornadoes-alabama-monday-wxc/index.html.

DoSomething.org. "11 Facts About Blizzards." Retrieved April 16, 2019. https://www.dosomething.org/us/facts/11-facts-about-blizzards.

Drimmer, Stephanie Warren. *National Geographic Kids Ultimate Weatherpedia: The Most Complete Weather Reference Ever.* Washington, DC: National Geographic Children's Books, 2019.

Edwards, Roger. "Tornado Safety." Storm Prediction Center. Retrieved April 16, 2019. https://www.spc.noaa.gov/faq/tornado/safety.html.

Griffey, Harriet. *Earthquakes and Other Natural Disasters.* New York, NY: DK Publishing, 2010.

Kostigen, Thomas M. *Extreme Weather: Surviving Tornadoes, Sandstorms, Hailstorms, Blizzards, Hurricanes and More!* Washington, DC: National Geographic Society, 2014.

Lewin, Lyric, Brett Roegiers, Bernadette Tuazon, and Kyle Almond. "In Pictures: Hurricane Maria Pummels Puerto Rico." CNN.com, September 2017. https://www.cnn.com/interactive/2017/09/world/hurricane-maria-puerto-rico-cnnphotos.

Livingston, Ian, and Kevin Ambrose. "Snowmageddon, Five years Later: The First of Two Mid-Atlantic Blizzards in February 2010." *Washington Post*. Retrieved March 15, 2019. https://www.washingtonpost.com/news/capital-weather-gang/wp/2015/02/04/snowmageddon-five-years-later-the-first-mid-atlantic-blizzard-of-february-2010/?outputType=comment&commentID=washingtonpost.com/ECHO/item/1423077533-482-657.

Lloyd, Jonathan. "Arson Suspect Charged in Cleveland National Forest Wildfire." NBC4 Los Angeles, August 8, 2018. https://www.nbclosangeles.com/news/local/Holy-Fire-California-Wildfires-Arrest-Riverside-Orange-Cleveland-National-Forest-490374161.html.

Mack, Eric. "See the Remarkably Stupid Moment Arizona's Sawmill Fire Was Started at a Gender Reveal Party." Forbes.com, August 17, 2019. https://www.forbes.com/sites/ericmack/2018/11/27/see-the-remarkably-stupid-moment-arizonas-sawmill-fire-was-started-at-a-gender-reveal-party.

National Resources Canada. "Canada's Ten Largest Earthquakes." Retrieved April 16, 2019. http://www.earthquakescanada.ca/pprs-pprp/pubs/GF-GI/GEOFACT_largest-earthquakes_e.pdf.

National Resources Canada. "What Is a Volcano?" July 13, 2018. http://chis.nrcan.gc.ca/volcano-volcan/volcano-volcan-en.php.

NOAA National Centers for Environmental Information (NCEI). "U.S. Billion-Dollar Weather and Climate Disasters (2019)." January 2019. https://www.ncdc.noaa.gov/billions.

NSSL. "Severe Weather 101: Tornado Basics." Noaa.gov. Retrieved April 16, 2019. https://www.nssl.noaa.gov/education/svrwx101/tornadoes.

Prendergast, Curt. "Border Agent to Pay $220K for Tucson-Area Wildfire Sparked at Gender-Reveal Party." *Arizona Daily Star*, September 20, 2018. https://tucson.com/news/local/border-agent-to-pay-k-after-starting-sawmill-fire-during/article_77b07742-c343-11e8-a6c7-9b739a2ac90b.amp.html?__twitter_impression=true.

Ready.gov. "Know the Facts: Earthquakes." Retrieved April 16, 2019. https://www.ready.gov/kids/know-the-facts/earthquakes.

Ready.gov. "Wildfires." Retrieved April 16, 2019. https://www.ready.gov/wildfires.

Roker, Al. *Al Roker's Extreme Weather: Tornadoes, Typhoons, and Other Weather Phenomena.* New York, NY: HarperCollins Publishers, 2017.

United States Geological Survey. "How Many Active Volcanoes Are There on Earth?" Retrieved April 16, 2019. https://www.usgs.gov/faqs/how-many-active-volcanoes-are-there-earth?qt-news_science_products=0#qt-news_science_products.

Watts, Claire. *Eyewitness Natural Disasters*. New York, NY: DK Publishing, 2015.

Weather Wiz Kids. "Landslide Questions." Retrieved April 16, 2019. https://www.weatherwizkids.com/?page_id=1326.

Index

A

American Red Cross, 28, 29

anger, 82

arson, 10–11, 75

avalanches, 9, 50–53, 55

B

blizzards, 4, 10, 46, 47–49, 52–53, 54–55

blood donation, 29

brush fires, 76, 78

burn ban, 10, 76

C

coastal flooding, 43

confusion, 88

cost/damages, 11–12, 13–14, 72–73

counseling/help from mental health professionals, 55, 81, 88, 91, 92, 96

crown fires, 77

Cullinane, Susannah, 8

curfews, 26

cyclones, 14, 38

D

debris flow, 14

depression, 55, 82

disabilities, people with, 55, 84–86

droughts, 4, 10, 13, 76

E

earthquakes, 16, 57–63, 85

emergency contacts, 86, 87–88

emergency kits, 45, 85

Enhanced Fujita scale, 66

evacuation, 15, 41–42, 43, 79–80

eye of a hurricane, 40–41

F

Facebook, 40

fear, 55, 82, 88

Federal Emergency Management Agency (FEMA), 26–28, 79

federal government, aid/help from, 23–24, 26–28, 33

fire-related careers, 74–75

firestorms, 77

fire triangle, 73
fire watch, 70
first responders, 23, 45, 86
flash floods, 43, 44
floods, 4, 9, 10, 42–44
food banks, 94–95
frustration, 88

H

hail, 63, 65
"Holy Fire," 74
hurricanes, 4, 6, 9, 10, 13, 34, 35–37, 38, 40–42, 43, 59, 63
hurricane season, 41

I

insomnia, 55

L

landslides, 4, 14–15
local government, aid/help from, 23–25, 33
low-income communities, 13

M

Mack, Eric, 71
Maria, Hurricane, 35–37
Mauna Loa, 16
Mercader, Carlos, 36
Modified Mercalli scale, 59–60
Mount St. Helens, 18
mudslides, 14, 15

N

National Aeronautics and Space Administration (NASA), 18
National Centers for Environmental Information (NCEI), 11–12, 13
National Oceanic and Atmospheric Administration (NOAA), 11–12, 38–40, 41, 63
National Weather Service, 65, 70
Natural Resources Canada, 15, 61
news/information, 5, 24, 25, 30–31, 38, 44, 49, 79, 87, 89

P

personal documents, protecting, 87

pets, 4, 18–20, 23, 44–45
post-traumatic stress disorder (PTSD), 84
Prendergast, Curt, 70
prescribed burns, 78–79

R

Richter scale, 59, 60
Roker, Al, 63

S

sadness, 82, 88, 96
San Andreas Fault Zone, 59
sandbags/sandbag walls, 43–44
"Sawmill Fire," 70
scams, 93
science project/science fairs, 17
seismologists, 59
self-care, purposeful, 88–94
self-harm, 91–92
"shelter in place," 67
smoke jumpers, 77
Snowmageddon, 46, 47
social media, 31, 39–40, 57, 87, 89–90
standing water, danger of, 34, 44
state government, aid/help from, 23–24, 26, 33
state of emergency, explanation of, 26
Sterling, Joe, 8
storm cellars, 67
storm surges, 43
Suicide Hotline, 92
supercells, 66–67
survivor's guilt, 82–83

T

tectonic plates, 59
Tornado Alley, 64
tornadoes, 4, 6, 8, 9, 10, 13, 63–69
tsunamis, 4, 16, 38, 57

U

US Geological Survey, 15, 16, 58, 59
United Way, 28

volcanoes, 4, 10, 14, 15–18

warnings and watches, 15, 38–40, 44, 48, 67, 70, 87

water bombers, 77

wildfires, 4, 9, 10, 14, 70–81

wildlife, 4, 18, 77

Youth Preparedness Council, 28

About the Author

A former corporate publications editor and writer, Lisa A. Crayton loves writing for children and teens—but she doesn't like snow! She toughed it out, though, while earning a bachelor's degree in public relations and journalism, cum laude, from Utica College, which is located in upstate New York, where it snowed seemingly nonstop in the fall and winter while she attended. Crayton is the author of a dozen other books for youth and the coauthor of six others. She loves mentoring writers and especially enjoys speaking at writers' conferences. Crayton earned a master of fine arts degree from National University.

Photo Credits

Cover Klaus Vedfelt/DigitalVision/Getty Images; p. 5 Pius Utomi Ekpei/AFP/Getty Images; p. 9 © AP Images; p. 12 Andrew Burton/Getty Images; p. 16 USGS; p. 19 Suzanne Cordeiro/AFP/Getty Images; p. 22 Marianne Todd/Getty Images; p. 25 Sandy Huffaker/Getty Images; p. 27 Walt Jennings/FEMA; p. 30 Brian Vander Brug/Los Angeles Times/Getty Images; p. 32 Brendan Smialowski/AFP/Getty Images; p. 36 NASA; p. 39 Brett Deering/Getty Images; p. 41 NOAA/JPL-Caltech; p. 43 Bull's-Eye Arts/Shutterstock.com; p. 47 Spencer Platt/Getty Images; p. 50 Roman Mikhailiuk/Shutterstock.com; p. 53 Sam Edwards/OJO Images/Getty Images; p. 54 Pitiya Phinjongsakundit/Shutterstock.com; p. 58 raditya/Shutterstock.com; p. 60 Designua/Shutterstock.com; p. 64 Chris Clor/Getty Images; p. 66 TinoFotografie/Shutterstock.com; p. 68 Scott Olson/Getty Images; p. 71 Simply Beautiful Photos/iStock /Getty Images; p. 72 Luciano Cosmo/Getty Images; p. 74 Robyn Beck/AFP/Getty Images; p. 78 Murphy_Shewchuk/iStock/Getty Images; p. 80 Nils Petersen/Getty Images; p. 83 9nong/Shutterstock.com; p. 85 Nicholas Kamm/AFP/Getty Images; p. 89 LightField Studios/Shutterstock.com; p. 91 Tim Hall/Cultura/Getty Images; p. 95 fstop123/E+/Getty Images.

Design: Michael Moy; Layout: Ellina Litmanovich; Editor: Erin Staley; Photo Researcher: Sherri Jackson